The Battle of Bosworth Field: The History of the Battle that Ended the Wars of the Roses

By Charles River Editors

Philip James de Loutherbourg's depiction of the Battle of Bosworth Field

About Charles River Editors

Charles River Editors provides superior editing and original writing services across the digital publishing industry, with the expertise to create digital content for publishers across a vast range of subject matter. In addition to providing original digital content for third party publishers, we also republish civilization's greatest literary works, bringing them to new generations of readers via ebooks.

Sign up here to receive updates about free books as we publish them, and visit Our Kindle Author Page to browse today's free promotions and our most recently published Kindle titles.

Introduction

Henry Payne's painting depicting people choosing between white roses and red roses

The Battle of Bosworth Field

"Near this spot, on August 22nd 1485, at the age of 32, King Richard III fell fighting gallantly in defence of his realm & his crown against the usurper Henry Tudor."

Today, roses are a sign of love and luxury, but for over 30 years, they provided the symbols for two houses at war for control of England. Thousands of people died and many more were injured fighting beneath the white rose of York and the red rose of Lancaster, and the noble families ruling England tore each other apart in a struggle that was as bitter as it was bloody. Though what followed was a period of strong rule under the Tudors monarchs, it ultimately came at a terrible cost, and even then, it was through Elizabeth of York that the Tudor line received its legitimacy. After all, while Henry VII won his throne in battle, Elizabeth of York was the daughter of King Edward IV of England, a Yorkist monarch.

Few battles in English history are as famous as Bosworth Field. Fought on August 22, 1485, it was the one which decided the outcome of that long and messy conflict. English king Richard

III, who had only recently taken the throne, had superior numbers at the battle, but an army fighting under future king Henry VII proved to have the better fighters. When forces near the field under Lord Stanley sided with Henry during the battle, they surrounded and killed Richard. The last York King went down fighting, but as news of the king's death spread, his army turned and ran, and with that, Henry Tudor was now King Henry VII.

Immortalized in drama by William Shakespeare and in comedy by Rowan Atkinson and Richard Curtis, the Battle of Bosworth Field has been a mainstay of British culture since the day it was fought. Meanwhile, excitement over the real history of the period reached a peak in late 2012 and early 2013 when Richard III's long-lost remains were found by archaeologists. The once proud king, who fell on the field at Bosworth, was found beneath a parking lot after the church in which he had been buried was destroyed. This provoked a new rash of books about Richard, as well as a dispute over where his remains should be reburied. Centuries later, passions can still run high about the conflict.

The Wars of the Roses are brought more literally to life by the hundreds of people who dress up in military costumes of the period and refight its battles in displays every summer. Both politically dramatic and visually interesting, the Wars of the Roses are one of the most popular periods for British reenactments. However, the most popular cultural response to the Wars of the Roses is not a work of history or historical fiction but one of fantasy; George R R Martin's Game of Thrones books, and their TV adaptation, are hugely influenced by the Wars of the Roses. Martin has taken the core of the conflict - a political and personal struggle between two medieval dynasties - and depicted it on an epic scale. Though his version contains monsters and magic, it also contains many incidents based on those of the war, as well as characters based on its protagonists, most notably the noble houses of Stark and Lannister. The Wars of the Roses may have ended centuries ago, but they clearly remain fascinating to this day.

The Battle of Bosworth Field: The History of the Battle that Ended the Wars of the Roses traces the history that led to Bosworth, and the battle that brought the Tudors to power. Along with pictures of important people, places, and events, you will learn about the Battle of Bosworth Field like never before, in no time at all.

The Battle of Bosworth Field: The History of the Battle that Ended the Wars of the Roses
About Charles River Editors
Introduction
   Chapter 1: Causes of the War
   Chapter 2: How the Battles Were Fought
   Chapter 3: The Brief Return of Henry VI
   Chapter 4: The Rise of Richard III
   Chapter 5: The Campaign
   Chapter 6: The Armies
   Chapter 7: Initial Maneuvers
   Chapter 8: The Climax
   Chapter 9: The Aftermath of the Battle
   Online Resources
   Bibliography

Chapter 1: Causes of the War

To understand the outbreak of the Wars of the Roses in 1455, it's necessary to go back more than half a century to the overthrow of King Richard II of England. Richard II was not a popular king. Having lost control of his country for two years to a group known as the Lords Appellant, on regaining power he eventually took revenge on them. Fearing that he might be usurped, in 1399 he exiled Henry of Bolingbroke, the son of his late Uncle the Duke of Lancaster, a potential claimant to the throne. Bolingbroke returned, rallied Richard's opponents and deposed him, taking the throne as King Henry IV, the first king of the House of Lancaster.

Richard II

Henry IV

Such political shifts were not uncommon in the Middle Ages, and Henry's swift, successful coup caused little disruption to the country; in fact, he and his descendants ruled relatively successfully for 50 years. However, the coup still created a weakness in the royal line, and it was a weakness that would eventually lead to war.

Since the Lancastrian kings were not descended from the central royal line and had only gained the throne by force, they lacked the legitimacy of some previous rulers. A series of unsuccessful revolts were planned against them, including one in 1415 that involved Richard, Duke of Cambridge, a younger brother of the Duke of York, and which led to Richard's execution for treason.

Henry IV's successor, Henry V, was a strong but short-lived king, and his early death in 1422 left his infant son Henry VI as monarch. As if that wasn't a big enough disadvantage, this Henry lacked the strength of his ancestors. Becoming king at the age of nine months, he was not able to rule in his own right for many years, and this led to a habit of listening to his advisers, who had a strong influence over him even as an adult. As with many kings, a group of favorites gathered around him, and by 1450 he was increasingly reliant on a single Lancastrian faction, to the exclusion of other voices at court.

Henry V

Henry VI

Throughout this period, England was at war with France in what is now known as the Hundred Years War, which had been running for decades as English kings tried to claim sovereignty over France while French kings tried to seize territory long held by the English. In 1417, Henry V launched another campaign, during which his brutal sacking of Caen led other French towns to surrender. With the Burgundians and Armagnacs at war with each other, he faced little opposition and conquered large swathes of northern France. He refortified captured settlements, set up his own administration, and replaced local nobles with loyal Englishmen.

However, the political landscape had shifted again in 1419 when the Armagnacs killed John of Burgundy at a peace meeting. The new duke, Philip the Good, sided with Henry against the increasingly discredited Armagnacs, who had the Dauphin, the French crown prince, on their side. Philip and Henry negotiated with the befuddled King Charles VI, who agreed to Henry marrying his daughter and becoming his heir. They then went on to capture Paris, which the English held for the next 15 years.

Just weeks after Henry V became ill and died on August 31, 1322, leaving his infant son as king, Charles VI also died. King Henry VI of England was now viewed by many as also being King Henry II of France, while on the French side Charles VII took the throne. In Henry VI's infancy, his French lands were ruled by his uncle John, the Duke of Bedford. Backed loyally by experienced English fighting nobility, and more tenuously by the Dukes of Burgundy and Brittany, he ruled large swathes of France on Henry's behalf, even occasionally extending his territory south.

Though the English had great successes on the battlefield, most notably at Agincourt in 1415, they were losing the war, and through a slow campaign of raids, sieges and local diplomacy, the French eventually pushed them back. This created two problems for young Henry VI. One was that the royal finances were exhausted, having been expended in years of warfare that had enriched individual nobles but impoverished the crown. The other problem, related to the first, was that there were deep political divisions about whether to continue the war. Many close to Henry argued that they should make peace with the French, ending a conflict that had been hugely costly in both money and lives, but others objected to giving up territory in France and the perceived dishonor of giving up on the fight. They believed, despite everything thus far, that England could win.

Medieval depiction of the Battle of Agincourt

As this once successful war turned slowly but inexorably into ignominious defeat, it had an impact beyond the royal court. Most significant was the state of the economy; the war was costly to fight, but as long as it was successful soldiers brought back wealth in the form of looted treasure and ransoms paid for the release of captured French knights. Once successes became few and far between, that source of income was gone, along with money from land once held in France. French success also disrupted English trade, and longstanding ties with the continent were broken.

Naturally, ordinary people became increasingly unhappy at their hardships, and into this volatile situation came the men who had fought the war, ordinary soldiers now out of work. Many had lost their source of income, as well as their sense of purpose, and they stirred up civil disturbances among the already unhappy English, creating a sense of turmoil in the country.

In the summer of 1453, the last significant English territory in France was lost when Bordeaux fell. Henry VI, never the most ruggedly healthy of kings, suffered a mental breakdown upon hearing the news, and a country in crisis now essentially found itself without a leader. Into the gap stepped Richard, Duke of York. The son of the Duke of Cambridge - the man executed by Henry's father in 1415 - Richard of York was also descended from King Edward III on both signs of his family, giving him a claim to the throne. A veteran of the war in France, he believed that his position there had been undermined by the political maneuvering of those around the King. Bitter and alienated, he had led unsuccessful political opposition to Henry since 1450, all while pushing to be recognized as Henry's heir.

Stained glass window depicting Richard, Duke of York

By October 1453, it was clear the Henry's illness would not pass quickly; silent and non-responsive, he was not engaging with the people around him. A Great Council was called to help govern, and the Duke of York, as the leading Duke in England, was a part of this. He quickly took control and had his political opponent, the Duke of Somerset, imprisoned in the Tower of London. Despite opposition from Queen Margaret of Anjou, on March 27, 1454 Richard was appointed Protector of the Realm and Chief Councillor. With that, he was effectively running England.

Margaret of Anjou

Richard of York was a stronger leader than Henry VI had ever been, but his rule proved short-lived. In January 1455, Henry VI regained his sanity and took control of the kingdom once more, after which he immediately started undoing everything the Duke of York had done, stripped the Duke of titles, and released Somerset from the Tower. By this point, however, York's period as Protector and the king's intervention in a dispute between the noble families of Percy and Neville had given Richard the one thing he had previously lacked: substantial support. Moreover, Somerset's closeness to the Percys cause brought the powerful Nevilles into York's camp.

Excluded from power, and with Margaret of Anjou and others in court plotting against him, York feared that he would be tried for treason. Politics had failed him, so he turned to his one remaining option for gaining power: recruiting an army for war.

Chapter 2: How the Battles Were Fought

The Wars of the Roses came at the end of the period that most perfectly fits the popular image of medieval warfare. Heavily armored knights fought alongside longbow-wielding archers, but the changes that marked Europe's military revolution were already starting to show. Infantry armed with polearms, always a reality of medieval warfare, formed a large part of the armies, and cannons and siege weapons had gone from rarities to a common sight on the field of battle. Handguns were also starting to make themselves known.

The military leaders in civil war, just as in international war, were the nobility. Men with lands, titles and political influence, they were used to being in charge, and they had an obligation to more senior lords and to the king to raise troops in times of war. Though that obligation was compromised by multiple claimants to the throne, it was still the backbone of the armies. Moreover, the concept of chivalry, a set of ideals built around military courage and correct behavior, had come to prominence in the previous century, and books on the subject were popular among the nobility. Heroic acts of violence were romanticized, and fighting for their king was thus an ideal to which many nobles aspired.

The rest of the soldiers were recruited by these nobles. The traditional feudal system gave men an obligation to fight for the nobles on whose land they lived, but by the Wars of the Roses England had entered a period known as bastard feudalism, where the strict ties of the traditional hierarchy were being undermined. Money, power and position were used to recruit lesser nobles and soldiers to each side, and local lords often kept bodies of troops ready. The increased power this gave individual nobles undermined the power of the king and contributed to the war.

The system through which these forces were maintained was known as livery and maintenance. A noble's followers would wear their symbols and colors to show their allegiance and in return receive the lord's protection, while troops of men-at-arms were maintained through pay.

Though many men fighting for a noble came through their household, some were mercenaries and others were hired from the local area. The ability to recruit therefore depended not only a leader's wealth and status but on the geographical location of their property.

People often picture knights and medieval warriors dressed from head to toe in plate armor, and while this was not true for much of the Middle Ages, by the 15th century it had become a reality. Armor-making technology had reached the point where it was possible to dress a man in an entire suit of plate, a form of protection previously available only to the wealthiest fighters. In this sense, the knights of the Wars of the Roses are knights as people today imagine them, clothed from head to toe in solid metal.

Though horses were used in warfare, the English mostly used them for transport rather than fighting from horseback. While Richard III would ride down Henry Tudor's men at the Battle of

Bosworth Field, there were other occasions when the most senior nobility got down from their armored horses and fought on foot, as Edward IV would do when he joined the front line at Towton. The rest of the soldiers, no matter how they traveled, fought as infantry. Like much in the English way of fighting, this had been shaped by the experience of the Hundred Years War. The great English successes of that war - Crécy, Poitiers and Agincourt - had all come down to the superiority of English infantry in the face of a French charge.

The Hundred Years War had also seen the rise of that most iconic English and Welsh weapon, the longbow. Bowmen were important in battle, as they were used to soften up the enemy before close combat or to force them to move from a good position, as would be the case at the Battle of Towton. Though advances in armor meant that arrows were less likely to penetrate the protection of a fully armored knight, they could still do so, and sheer volume of arrows could put pressure on enemy formations.

It was fighting at close quarters that decided the outcome of the war's battles, and in that the majority of the fighters were not heavily armored knights but the infantrymen serving them. The equipment of these men was similar to that used by ordinary infantry throughout the Middle Ages; they were usually armed with long weapons such as bills and spears, giving them extra reach, as well as smaller weapons for when the fighting got up close. Their armor depended on their wealth and circumstances, from humble padded jackets to pieces of plate like those worn by their leaders. Most wore helmets to protect their heads, and they fought in large groups, creating a bristling wall of spear points that could be hard to penetrate and which was the precursor of the pike formations that would soon become important.

Though not yet a dominant battlefield force, handguns were starting to be seen on the battlefield. These were primitive firearms compared with those of later centuries, but they had the main advantage that would make firearms so popular: ease of use. Effectively pointing and firing a gun at a mass of enemy troops didn't take the years of training involved in making a bowman or good fighter. Neither the gunners nor the guns even needed to be very accurate; they relied on firing into massed blocks of enemy troops, easier to hit than a barn door.

Handguns had been preceded onto the battlefield by cannons, and the armies of the Wars of the Roses, like some of those in the Hundred Years War, had artillery trains that they took to battle, though the fast moving nature of the Wars of the Roses meant they were used less heavily than in some contemporary conflicts. Cannons were used to bombard the enemy at long range, and their ammunition has been found by archaeologists littering battlefields of the period. Gunpowder did not yet dominate warfare, but the roar of the guns, the clouds of smoke and the terrifying devastation these weapons could bring were all present in what remained a very medieval war.

The Hundred Years War, a conflict that ended right around the beginning of the Wars of the Roses, had been fought mostly through sieges. In a struggle for control of territory, the two sides fought a long, slow war in which months at a time were spent vying for control of individual towns and castles. The English lost the war despite winning its greatest battles because they lost that grinding campaign of siege and local struggle.

Conversely, the Wars of the Roses were fought in a far different style. Though the Siege of Harlech lasted from 1460-1468 as Margaret of Anjou and other Lancastrians held out against the victorious royalists, sieges were a rarity. The opposing sides were fighting not for territory but for legitimacy and the right to rule, so sieges and sackings would have destroyed property they already claimed as their own. Thus, the war was about fast maneuvering and pitched battles, with each side trying to defeat the other while they thought they had the advantage in numbers or had to make their political point. Though the nobles fighting the wars maintained bands of soldiers in their households, whole armies were not kept in the field for extended periods, and the rush to gather an army was the first stage of most campaigns.

The treatment of enemy leaders was also different from international conflicts such as the Hundred Years War or the Scottish border wars. When fighting another country, medieval warriors tried to take the opposing nobility captive so that they could ransom them back to their families at a profit. However, in a civil war, the nobles of the two sides were competing for the same positions of power and control of the same estates. In victory, they would be seizing property and power from their opponents anyway, so there was no need to sell them back to make a profit. Besides, they didn't want those opponents around competing for the same positions in court. The result was a war in which battles were more prominent, but ransomed captives, the common outcome of battles in the Hundred Years War, almost never happened.

Such all-or-nothing outcomes were reinforced, especially under Richard III, by the use of treason laws. These provided an excuse to execute captured opponents in a way that was not acceptable when fighting a foreign nation. Between the threat of treason trials, the death of opponents in custody, and the reduced motive to take prisoners in battle, it is little wonder that defeated leaders chose exile rather than risk their lives by fighting to the finish or surrendering to their opponents.

Chapter 3: The Brief Return of Henry VI

In the winter of 1470-71, the position of the Lancaster king Henry VI and his wife Margaret of Anjou must have looked like a strong one. Henry was once again free after years of imprisonment, and Margaret was home after years of exile. Their initial opponent, Richard of York, was dead, and his son, Edward IV, was in exile. Furthermore, the one figure connecting all the major Yorkist successes, the Earl of Warwick, had come over to their side, and even Edward's own brother, the Duke of Clarence, had chosen to back the Lancasters.

However, many of the signs of victory were also warnings of the problems they faced. First and foremost was the challenge of reconciling their different supporters; Warwick's power and prestige were based on the losses of longstanding Lancastrian supporters, making it impossible to reward both groups in the ways they hoped for. For his part, Clarence was also a mixed blessing. He had originally rebelled against his brother because he was arrogant enough to believe that the act might make him king. Of course, with a different family on the throne and his brother in exile, that looked less realistic than ever, and to make his position worse, he had already shown himself unreliable in his loyalties. Though he had cast his lot with the Lancasters, they understood he had even less reason to stay loyal to them than he had to his brother.

Then there was Edward of York, still claiming the title King Edward IV. As long as two kings of England lived, neither of them could feel secure, and Edward had shown himself to be a capable leader, willing to retreat when necessary but more than capable of going on the offensive. Having escaped to the continent, he sought support from his brother-in-law Charles the Bold, Duke of Burgundy, a man with as much wealth and influence as some European kings, and upon whom Warwick had declared war.

Edward IV

Charles the Bold

Together with other English nobles who had fled with him into exile, and with support from both Charles the Bold and merchants from the Low Countries, Edward quickly assembled an army and invasion fleet. It wasn't a large army - 1,200 men in 36 ships - but Edward didn't want to give his enemies time to consolidate their power. On March 11, 1471, he set sail, and after being blown off course, he landed at Ravenspur at the mouth of the River Humber, the same place where Henry Bolingbroke had landed to seize the country 72 years before.

Gathering supporters as he marched south, Edward benefited from the other weakness of

Henry VI's restored regime: the king's unpopularity. When Edward had been ruling and not doing exactly what they wanted, people had quickly forgotten the reasons why they had put him on the throne in the first place, but Henry's return immediately reminded them that he had been a weak king who was dominated by favorites and incapable of leading in his own right. Henry's weakness had been a prime cause of the violent lawlessness during his previous reign, so after only a few months in which Warwick and Margaret ruled in Henry's name, many people were ready to support Edward once more.

In hindsight, it's easy to be critical of the endless switching of sides going on during the era, but that's hardly new in politics. Some people would support a candidate up until they became king, then side with the opposition when they didn't like what that king did. All the while, riots and rebellions were major means of political expression during the Middle Ages since there were no elections for people to participate in and few opportunities for most to vent their discontent. Thus, when the opportunity came, they took it.

To his credit, the Duke of Clarence tried at first to support his recent allies by gathering troops for Warwick, but when confronted in April by an increasingly powerful Edward, he switched back to his brother's side. Having reconciled with Clarence and failed to draw Warwick into a battle, Edward marched on London. The capital was the heart of England's economy and government, a great trading port and administrative center. Its merchants had previously lent large sums of money to Edward, and they had little reason to oppose his return, which promised them a brighter financial future. He was easily able to take the city, including the Tower of London, and poor Henry VI along with it. It is hard to tell what to make of Henry telling Edward, on meeting him once again as his captive, that he felt safe in his hands. Was this an attempt to pressure Edward into treating him well, a reflection of his previous survival in prison, or the rambling of a broken mind? Whatever the case, the words would prove tragically mistaken.

Warwick, who had previously holed up in Coventry, was now on the march. Hoping to catch Edward in the open outside London, he was thwarted by the welcoming reception Londoners gave the returning king. Warwick had the superior numbers, so Edward's best hope lay in using speed and surprise. He marched out of the city, bringing Henry with him in the hope that the Lancastrians would avoid attacking the king.

The two armies met a few miles north of London, and the Battle of Barnet, fought on April 14, 1471, was one of the most important of the war. Thick fog forced the two armies to rely on close quarter fighting and made it hard to tell what was happening. This contributed to a mistake in which Lancastrian troops attacked each other. Believing they had been betrayed, morale plummeted and the Lancastrians fled. Warwick was pursued, captured, and killed by Yorkist soldiers, and several other leading men died on both sides.

An illustration depicting the Battle of Barnet

On the same day that battle was joined at Barnet, Margaret of Anjou arrived in England at Weymouth, along with her and Henry's only son, Prince Edward of Westminster. Warwick's defeat left them without their most significant bloc of support, so rather than confront King Edward, they headed toward Wales, gathering support along the way. Realizing that they intended to link up with supporters in Wales and that the mountainous region would be easier for them to defend, the Yorkist king marched west to cut them off before they crossed the River Severn, the boundary between England and Wales.

Both armies marched quickly, but King Edward was able to intercept the Lancastrians just before they could make a crossing. They retreated to Tewkesbury, and it was there that the two forces fought on May 4. Once again, King Edward was outnumbered, but this time he had significant advantages; more of his troops had travelled by horse rather than on foot, leaving them better rested, and they were better equipped with artillery. A flanking force of Lancastrians under the Duke of Somerset was itself flanked by a group of spearmen Edward had placed on his left, so in the battle, Somerset's force was routed and the Lancastrians ran. Prevented from fleeing by the small River Swilgate, many were hacked to pieces, and Prince Edward was captured and killed by the Duke of Clarence's men. Many of the surviving Lancastrian leaders were summarily tried and executed two days later, and Margaret of Anjou surrendered herself soon after that.

Only one more Lancastrian force remained in the field. This one was led by Thomas Neville, also known as the Bastard of Fauconberg, a veteran of the Hundred Years War. Fauconberg attacked London on May 14 but was driven back by the Yorkist garrison and Londoners intent on defending their property. Hearing of the defeat at Tewkesbury and that Edward's army was approaching, Fauconberg retreated, and he soon after gave up the fight. Five months later, he was executed for attempting to escape custody.

Three Lancastrian armies had been raised, and all had been defeated by King Edward and his followers. Only one loose end remained: Henry VI. Once again a prisoner in the Tower of London, he had been useful to the Yorkists as long as his son was still alive because his survival prevented the stronger Prince Edward from claiming the throne. Upon the Prince's death at Tewkesbury, however, Henry was now a liability since he might serve as a rallying point for Lancastrian resistance.

After facing repeated revolts, Edward IV was apparently feeling less merciful than before. Henry died on the night May 21, 1471, presumably on Edward's orders. The poor mad king, so long a pawn in others' struggles, died an ignominious death in a prison cell.

The very next day, Edward IV was once again proclaimed king.

Chapter 4: The Rise of Richard III

With Edward IV in power again, England now saw a period of relative tranquility, and some scholars even consider this the end of the Wars of the Roses proper, with the later violence a postscript to the real conflict. However, it was this later violence that brought about the Battle of Bosworth Field and ended the feud between Lancaster and York, and which saw the names of both noble houses relegated to the history books, so stopping in 1471 doesn't see the conflict through to its bitter end.

That said, there were no more great rebellions during Edward IV's reign. Since the death of

Prince Edward left Henry VI without children, and Henry himself had been an only son, the Lancastrians had to look far afield for a new claimant to the throne around whom they could galvanize their support. Though not the most legitimate claimant given that his royal connection involved both a woman and an illegitimate heir, Henry Tudor would become the head of the cause. However, with such a tenuous claim, and with opposition having been so effectively crushed at Barnet and Tewkesbury, it would be years before Henry Tudor became relevant.

Henry Tudor, the future King Henry VII, as a young man

In the meantime, Edward IV ruled as peacefully as could be expected of a medieval monarch, which is to say that he made war on his neighbors instead of his subjects. Having relied on Charles the Bold of Burgundy for support against Henry VI, Edward allied with him again for a planned invasion of France in 1485, a continuation of English royal attempts to lay claim to the French throne. Charles failed to provide the support Edward needed, and the invasion ended not in military glory but in a negotiated peace. In the end, Edward was paid off by the French, making back the money spent on the expedition, and this failure by Charles left the French King free to attack Burgundy without English intervention.

In 1482, Edward turned his eye north, backing the Duke of Albany's attempt to claim the throne of Scotland. English forces led by Edward's brother, Richard, Duke of Gloucester, invaded Scotland, seized Edinburgh and captured the Scottish king, but yet again, the English were let down by their allies. Albany reneged on the agreement he had made with them, and Gloucester withdrew. The only significant outcome for the English was that they took control of Berwick-upon-Tweed.

The Scottish campaign was indicative of the way Edward ruled. He used strong men loyal to him to enforce his will and was willing to make a show of force when the occasion called for it. Display was also the order of the day at court, where Edward made an ostentatious show of kingship. He wore the most fashionable clothes and jewelry, and he furnished the court in the latest style. He gathered a great collection of books, including ones on great leaders, and though he read for both education and pleasure, the spectacular illumination of many of these books shows that they also played a part in his great display. Together, these pieces paint a picture of a king working hard to reinforce his authority. He had risen to the throne through blood, and that left the legitimacy of his rule questionable. By asserting the authority and majesty of kingship, he reinforced his royal status in the minds of those around him.

Warwick's fall had also given Edward what he needed to richly reward his chief lieutenants, and he took care to do so. The late Earl's lands were divided up, with significant portions going to Edward's staunch ally William, Lord Hastings, and the King's loyal brother Richard of Gloucester. The Duke of Clarence, despite his betrayal, was given lands and some authority in the Midlands, a reward for the unconvincing but important display of loyalty he had made during Edward's campaign to retake the crown. Even still, the hot-headed Clarence could still not be trusted, becoming involved in violent and disruptive crimes, and when he fell out of favor with Edward, he lacked the will or focus to make a bid for the crown. He was eventually convicted of treason and executed in February 1478. Legend claims that he was drowned in a vat of wine.

Richard of Gloucester, the future King Richard III

The power and authority given to his close lieutenants allowed Edward to bring peace and stability after years of disruption and violence, but by empowering Gloucester, it would also sow the seeds for the final phase of the Wars of the Roses: Richard's seizure of the throne and the final overthrow of the House of York.

Edward IV fell ill at Easter 1483 after coming back from a fishing trip, and he died shortly after on April 9. What exactly killed him is unclear, and though some people would later speculate that he had been poisoned, there is every reason to believe that he died of natural causes. Disease was common in medieval England, and doctors lacked much of the medical knowledge now taken for granted. The King's spectacular lifestyle had taken its toll, and he was significantly overweight, so it seems the lifestyle which he thought he had earned as King, and which he used to remind everyone of his status, was probably his undoing.

Either way, Edward's death was ill timed. The previous year's campaign had created tensions with Scotland to little benefit, and France and Burgundy had made peace, ending the traditional diplomatic maneuver of playing those two countries off against each other. The example of Henry VI had shown that a child king could be incredibly dangerous for the country, and Edward's heir, Prince Edward, was only 12 years old. His other son, Richard, was just 10.

Given the circumstances, there was every likelihood that peace and stability would now come to an end, and that's precisely what happened. Given time and a more fitting rise to the throne, Edward V might have been a great king. Certainly, Edward IV's heir had been raised by a fine example of what a nobleman could be, though not by his father. Instead, he was tutored by his uncle and guardian, Anthony Woodville, Earl Rivers. Rivers was one of the most highly regarded knights in the country, a pious and chivalrous military veteran. He had supported William Caxton, the merchant who brought the first printing press to England, and he was a supportive guardian whose presence reassured the dying king. His position of trust running the young Edward's household now put him in a hugely powerful position as the most trusted adviser of a 12 year old king.

Recognizing that death was coming, the 40 year old Edward IV had tried to make arrangements for how the kingdom would be ruled during his son's minority. His aim was for Rivers to continue running the young king's household while Richard, Duke of Gloucester, became protector and took responsibility for running the country until Edward V was old enough to do so for himself. It was an arrangement designed to prevent any one person from gaining total authority during his son's childhood reign, and thus to protect the young king.

Richard was the only realistic candidate to become Protector in a royal minority. The late king's only surviving brother and one of his most effective and loyal lieutenants, he was also third in line to the throne after his young nephews. Of course, it was an arrangement that clearly appealed to the 30 year old Duke of Gloucester. At the time of his brother's death, he was busy defending the north of England, work which had made him popular in the region. He went to York for a ceremony to mourn his brother, but did not immediately travel south to join the royal councillors debating the future of the realm. Instead, he wrote to have them make him protector, and he had Lord Hastings campaign on his behalf.

However, the Queen's Woodville relatives, and many royal councillors, had other ideas. After extensive discussions, the Council declared that Edward V would rule as king in his own right from the start, just as if he were an adult, with the support by a council selected to advise him. Gloucester would be part of that council, but he would not have the preeminent position his brother had intended.

At first, everything seemed to be going smoothly, but behind the scenes Richard was scheming. As Edward V and his guardian Rivers were travelling toward London, Richard and his substantial military retinue met them on the road. After setting Rivers and another adviser at ease through a pleasant dinner on April 29, Richard showed his true colors the next day by taking them captive and taking control of the King. His justification was the old classic of protecting a king from evil advisers, this time in the form of the Woodvilles, but even his 12 year old nephew could see through the charade.

Arriving in London on May 4, 1483, Richard was made Protector five days later, and he had Edward's coronation postponed until June 22. The Queen withdrew, effectively going into hiding, while Gloucester tried unsuccessfully to make a case for Rivers and others among the king's retinue to be tried for treason. Those associated with the Woodville cause were scattered, arrested and in some cases executed, with Gloucester's former representative Hastings being among those to die after he wavered in his support.

All the while, Richard of Gloucester was backing himself into a corner. Whether or not his initial intention was to become king, his efforts to protect his family fortunes and follow his brother's will had now left him in a difficult position. When his nephew officially became king, the young Edward V was likely to punish Gloucester for his actions, thus ensuring the victory of the Woodvilles. In other words, coronation day held more threat than promise, so Gloucester had Edward V imprisoned in the Tower of London, where he was joined by his brother Richard on 16.

June 22 brought not a coronation but a scandal. Having cancelled the ceremony days beforehand, Gloucester instead had a theologian present the case that Edward IV had been contracted to marry someone else when he married Elizabeth Woodville, thus making his children illegitimate and unable to inherit the throne. It was a spurious argument, but it gave Gloucester's coup a thin layer of legitimacy. Three days later, it was announced that Gloucester would take the throne as King Richard III. Even as the announcement was made, Rivers and others of Edward V's advisers were being tried for treason and condemned to death.

It is easy to see why many nobles fell in line behind Richard III's coup. A child king could be a cause of great instability, something that was greatly feared after the bloodshed of previous decades. Moreover, Richard was well respected and had proven his political and military leadership. However ruthless his methods, many breathed a sigh of relief at seeing him become king.

The chain of events also contributed to one of England's most enduring mysteries. The young princes Edward and Richard never emerged from the Tower of London; like Henry VI before them, their very existence was a threat to the King's position and national stability. Unlike Henry, it's still not known when or how they died, but over the summer of 1483, fewer and fewer reports were heard of them. Everyone knew the ugly truth of what would happen, or perhaps by then what had already happened, but nobody wanted to express it out loud. As such, the Princes in the Tower simply faded into memory. It is possible that they died of illness or were killed on the orders of someone other than Richard III, but given everything that came before, Richard III remains the prime suspect in his young nephews' deaths.

The Two Princes Edward and Richard in the Tower, **1483** by Sir John Everett Millais

Though he is often portrayed as a sly villain, and his rise to the throne can easily be seen that way, there was far more to Richard III than a hunger for power. There were good reasons why many people supported him, just as there were good reasons why many opposed him. Divisions between northern and southern England are as old as the country itself, and by the 15th century it was possible to see them starting to fall into their modern form. The south, containing London and close connections with continental Europe, became the center of the nation's economic and political life. Those running England were likely to spend most of their time in the south, and this was where the majority of the more prosperous and outward-looking English lived. The north sometimes seemed neglected by comparison, being less economically prosperous and suffering the effects of Scottish border wars.

Edward IV's solution was the Council of the North. A body answering to the King, this Council had its own budget and officials, as well as the authority to govern northern England. Its existence implicitly acknowledged that the north was too far away to be effectively governed from London, and it was intended to give the government greater control of this often troubled region. From the time when it was founded in 1472, Richard led the Council. Already holding large lands in northern England, and with official power as his brother's representative there, he was an economic and political force to be reckoned with. He was also popular with many in the north, especially in York, an important economic, religious and administrative center. Not only did he help to enforce law and order, but he led armies against the perceived menace of Scotland, making him a hero to many northerners.

Thus, upon becoming king, Richard III had the support of several different groups - his regional supporters in northern England; opponents of the Woodvilles who did not want them to become more powerful; and some who looked back nervously on what had happened under previous child kings.

Though he was not king for long, Richard set about the business with speed and vigor, using his experiencing governing part of the country to help him run the whole. Some of his reforms were aimed at helping the poor, setting up a Court of Requests to help them have their grievances listened to. Others were aimed at the upper and middle classes, with the end of certain restrictions on the printing and sale of books and the translation of England's laws from their traditional French into English, increasing the accessibility of learning and the law. Whether from ideals or from a cynical desire to shore up his uncertain support, Richard was doing good things.

None of this could wash away the stain of a rise to power grounded not just in infanticide but, perhaps worse to some medieval minds, in regicide, the murder of a king. However, while outrage at these circumstances might provide an excuse for rebellion against Richard, the underlying reasons for resentment were more prosaic, and more in keeping with the events of the previous decades. The factional struggles among the English aristocracy that had put Richard in line to take the throne also made resentment against his rule inevitable.

When Richard took the throne, he was not seizing power from Edward V so much as he was taking it from his nephew's Woodville family and their associates. Richard purged many of his most prominent opponents, using show trials and executions to get rid of such influential figures as Earl Rivers, but he could not completely eradicate a faction who had for years played a dominant role at court, and whose patronage and power had bought them as many supporters as Richard himself had. On top of this, Richard's focus on maintaining his support in the north left many southerners disconnected from their new king, leaving the areas closer to London as a potential source of trouble.

This trouble first reared its head as early as July 1483, when a plot to burn part of London and release the princes from the Tower (though it was unclear if they were still alive) was uncovered and thwarted. However, the first serious revolt came near the end of the year. The Duke of Buckingham had long been one of Richard's firmest allies. His reasons for rebelling are unclear, but seem to have been about furthering his own power. What is known is that by September 1483 he had allied himself with the Woodville faction and was reaching out to Henry Tudor, the Lancastrian claimant to the throne, seeking support from this exiled would-be monarch. Buckingham's rebellion relied on coordinating three groups of rebels - an army he was raising in Wales and the bordering Marches, men from the habitually rebellious southern county of Kent, and forces led by Henry Tudor, which would sail to England from Brittany (where Henry had the support of the Breton Prime Minister).

Duke of Buckingham

Unfortunately for the Duke, no part of this plan went well, least of all the coordination. The Kentish rebellion started early and was quickly repressed, while strong winds prevented Henry Tudor from reaching England. Buckingham's efforts at recruitment were hampered by bad weather, which then blighted his army as it marched out in October. It quickly became apparent that the whole endeavor was falling apart. Buckingham abandoned what remained of his army and went into hiding, only to be handed over to Richard's side by a supposed friend on November 1 and executed for treason the next day.

Buckingham's revolt may have failed, but it achieved something that would be crucial for the history of England by uniting the Lancastrian and Woodville Yorkist factions behind a single plan. They now aimed to make Henry Tudor king, with Elizabeth of York, Edward V's older sister, as his queen. The feud between the houses and Lancaster and York, which had for so long kept the flames of war alive, was now a thing of the past. Richard III had the advantage of kingship, but his side was a faction within a faction, with even apparently loyal supporters turning against him.

Elizabeth of York

Personal tragedy and political setback combined against Richard on April 9, 1484 when his son Prince Edward died after a short illness. As Richard's only legitimate son, and therefore his only potential direct heir, Edward had been essential to ensuring Richard's position; after all, what good was a royal line if there was no one to inherit it? Richard thus faced not just personal heartbreak but the knowledge that his position had become less secure.

An able politician, Richard was still working to consolidate his hold on the throne. He undermined Henry Tudor's support on the continent by offering his own military support to the Bretons in exchange for Henry's extradition. But Henry was no fool either. He fled to Paris and into the welcoming arms of another of Richard's opponents, the French government.

There, from across the English Channel, Henry Tudor eyed up the Kingdom of England.

Chapter 5: The Campaign

European history is full of exiled nobles gathering in foreign courts and plotting their return to power. Centuries later, the French aristocracy would be the exiles following their country's revolution, but in the 1480s they were the hosts, providing a home to Henry Tudor and other disenfranchised English nobles. Indeed, a base of operations like the French court was important to Henry. As other persons of note left Richard's court in fear or disillusionment, they came to him, as did the support of French courtiers who wanted to prevent an Anglo-Breton alliance. From the French point of view, Henry was a way of influencing English foreign policy; if they supported him and helped him take the English crown, then they could reasonably expect England to be their friend.

An alliance with the French also brought the Scots over to Henry's side. Scotland and France were bound together by the "auld alliance", a treaty first agreed in 1295 by which the two countries agreed to support each other militarily against the English. Having been invaded by Richard when he was running the north for his brother, the Scots had every reason to see him as an enemy, and to join the French in placing a new king on the English throne.

For Richard, the buildup to Bosworth began in 1484 as he prepared for Henry to arrive, but staying ready for the inevitable invasion drained Richard's resources. He was forced to take out loans from his subjects to pay for the war effort, in particular the equipment his army would need. Nonetheless, by December 1484, Richard's spies were reporting that the invasion would definitely come in the following year, as Henry was gathering a fleet. Thus, Richard spent the first five months of 1485 in London, coordinating the defense of his realm from there and ensuring that there were local nobles and lookouts ready for any sign of invasion. Beacons were set up on hilltops to quickly carry the warning of any invasion.

Leaving London in mid-May, the King traveled north and arrived a month later in Nottingham, a central position from which he could quickly descend on any part of the country Henry chose to invade. Richard was ready and waiting.

Henry, meanwhile, was reliant on foreign backers to build an army and provide a fleet with which to sail to England. In exile at the court of the French King Charles VIII, he could count on some support from the French and the Scots, both of whom were happy to see England in turmoil and to seek Richard's removal from the throne. At the same time, however, Henry was hardly their highest priority and he struggled to muster the men and money he needed, so he was unable to launch the expected invasion of 1484.

Charles VIII of France

It was not until August 1, 1485 that Henry Tudor finally set sail from France and the campaign began in earnest. Henry landed on August 7, near Milford Haven in Wales, and as he arrived at sunset on St Anne's Head at the edge of Milford Haven, he knelt, held up his hands toward the sky, and quoted from Psalm 43: "Judge me, O Lord, and defend my cause." With him was a small force consisting largely of French and Scottish soldiers. He had around 4,000 mercenaries and a few hundred other English exiles, including leading Lancastrians and some former Yorkists who backed Henry because they opposed Richard.

The choice of south Wales as a starting point was quite deliberate. Henry had been born in Wales and had strong family ties in that country, and the region had traditionally supported the Lancastrians whose cause he now led, so it was potentially fertile ground for growing his army. Though Richard had ordered men in the region to act against invaders, when Henry Tudor and his army appeared, opposition melted away, and some went over to Henry's side, either out of pragmatism or loyalty to Henry's uncle Jasper Tudor, the former Earl of Pembroke.

Henry marched quickly up the west coast and then struck inland, across the center of Wales, which allowed him to avoid South Wales, a region containing more of Richard's supporters. This way, he also increased the chances of recruiting more supporters, and despite rumors of an opposing force in Cardigan, he found nobody standing in his way. He passed through there and Newtown, sending out letters as he went in search of support. He picked up what men he could while keeping up a fast pace, hoping to attack Richard before the king could finish mustering his forces.

Richard was at his hunting lodge at Bestwood near Nottingham when word of the invasion reached him on August 11. He had the strategic advantage of being King of England, with some forces already assembled and the ability to call on most of the country for troops. He had known of the imminent invasion since June, and he had his followers on high alert. Commissioners of array had also been put in place to recruit troops, allowing him to quickly gather a sizable army, and he was ready to send messages at speed throughout the country.

The importance of this level of organization is demonstrated by how quickly word spread to Richard's supporters around the country. For news of an invasion in south Wales to have reached him in Nottingham less than four days is impressive, and even more amazingly, in an era when the speed of detailed communication was limited to the fastest horse and rider, word of the invasion and Richard's need for troops reached key supporters in East Anglia by August 16, only a week after the invasion.

Messages were sent all over the country ordering troops to assemble at Nottingham on 16 August. While many could not have made this deadline, Richard's supporters acted quickly to rally to his cause - after all, their power and influence were tied to those of the King. Nottingham became a bustle of activity, as men and equipment were assembled, messengers coming and going in every direction.

One person was notably absent from Nottingham, and he would be the one who ultimately decided the fate of the kingdom: Thomas Lord Stanley. Hugely influential in north Wales and northwest England, the Stanley family held power in a region of strategic importance, especially given Henry Tudor's Welsh connections. On January 13, 1485, Richard had sent out orders to the men of north Wales to make themselves available for recruitment by Lord Stanley and his brother, Sir William Stanley, Justice of North Wales. Aside from their wealth and political influence, the Stanley family held land in a region known for its hardy warriors, and Richard intended for them to contribute to fighting off the rebels. That said, it was a risky decision, because Stanley, like many noble families, tended to act as a single political unit, and their leader was a pragmatist who in previous conflicts had avoided committing to a side until he knew who would win. It was a strategy he would follow once more.

Thomas Lord Stanley

Sir William Stanley

Lord Stanley had been with Richard earlier in the summer as he made his initial preparations to defend the kingdom, and by July, Stanley was back in Lancashire to govern his lands and recruit men for Richard's cause. Though the exact narrative of the Stanley family's activities during this period is debated, it is clear that Richard, aware of the Lord's checkered past, had doubts about his loyalties. As a result, he insisted that Lord Stanley's son George, Lord Strange, remain with the King. Strange, already in his 20s and a knight in his own right, became a hostage in all but name; if Lord Stanley rebelled, the consequences could be fatal for his son and heir.

When news of the invasion arrived, Richard wrote to Lord Stanley ordering his return to Nottingham, but Stanley said that he could not, as he had contracted the sweating sickness then afflicting many in England. Meanwhile, Lord Strange was caught trying to sneak away from Nottingham, and in pleading for mercy he confessed to being part of a conspiracy to support the rebels, together with his uncle Sir William Stanley and Lord Stanley's nephew John Savage. Having begged Richard for mercy, he wrote to his father asking him to bring forces as quickly as possible to join the King. William Stanley was declared a traitor, and any pretence that Strange was at court voluntarily was now at an end.

As Richard struggled to gain Stanley's support, no one moved to stop Henry as he headed east toward England and the king. He emerged into the Marches, the border region where Wales and England joined, arriving at Shrewsbury on the River Severn on August 17. The Welsh Gate, at which Henry and his international army arrived, was locked against him by the burgesses, doubtless influenced as much by fear of this horde of armed foreigners as by the loyalty many of them felt to King Richard. This was a problem for Henry; he didn't want to get drawn into besieging a town populated by the people he claimed to rule, but if Shrewsbury wouldn't let him in, other towns might follow its lead. He therefore entered into negotiations with the town's leaders, which eventually resulted in his army being allowed to march peacefully through the town.

In fact, the negotiations were aided by an emissary of the locally based Sir William Stanley. Henry had received a promise of support from the Stanley's, who, aside from being a powerful power family, controlled a lot of the territory through which the rebels planned to march. But even at this point, with his son captive, his brother declared a traitor and the armies on the move, Lord Stanley hedged his bets. He gathered an army but didn't join Henry Tudor, instead shadowing the rebels' journey out of the Marches and into the heart of England.

Marching on toward the Midlands, Henry picked up more troops in small groups as he went. Two of the largest additions were an estimated 400-500 men under Gilbert Talbot and 800 under Sir Richard Corbet, a stepson of Sir William Stanley. In a campaign like this, there were inevitably relatives on both sides, and Corbet's presence may indicate his own commitment or may be another sign of the Stanley's carefully treading a middle path by supporting Henry without committing themselves. Indeed, the delicacy with which the Stanley's maintained this balance was demonstrated on August 19 when Sir William Stanley met with Henry at Stafford and assured him that he would, in time, bring troops to support Henry. By this point, Sir William had already been declared a traitor by Richard, so he seemingly had nothing to lose by siding with Henry, yet he still would not commit his forces by joining Tudor's army. Furthermore, it is telling that it was Sir William, politically the junior of the Stanley leaders, and not Lord Thomas who met with Henry; it appears that they were providing enough reassurance so that they could say afterwards that they had always been on Henry's side, while never committing so decisively that they couldn't turn around and side with Richard.

For his part, King Richard couldn't wait long before confronting Henry. Throughout the Wars of the Roses, power lay with whoever could prove they were in control, so Richard needed to stifle the rebellion quickly. On August 19, he marched his army in battle formation from Nottingham to Leicester, where they were met by reinforcements from East Anglia and London. Others, including the significant muster of troops from York, were slower in arriving and would not reach Richard in time to take part in the campaign. The absence of the Stanley's, whose forces Richard still hoped to see on his side, was also a worry.

The invaders were now marching southeast, either intending to take London or making a feint of heading toward the capital as a way of outmaneuvering Richard. Whichever the case, all the armies were getting close to each other, including Henry's rebel invaders, Richard's loyalists, and two Stanley forces under Lord Stanley and Sir William. By this point the Stanley troops, which together would make an army several thousand strong, were always ahead of Henry on his march. If Henry asked, they could say they were with him, and if Richard asked, they could say they were fleeing or harassing the rebel army. Their uncertain loyalty even came close to ending Henry's invasion on the night of August 20 when he became separated from his army. Whether lost in thought out of concern at which way the Stanley's would go, as the record later suggested, or considering fleeing because of Richard's strength and the lack of Stanley support, Henry ended the day several miles from his main force. Even if this was just an accident, word of his absence could have led to the disintegration of his army if it had leaked out, but his officers covered for him, and the next day he was back with his men.

Arriving in Atherstone on August 20, Henry's army was finally allowed to rest after two weeks on the move. They stayed in camp near Atherstone for two nights, with the Stanley armies taking up two separate camps within a few miles of them. At Atherstone, Henry met with the Stanley leaders, and while the discussion was cordial, it did not result in a clear plan for how the Stanley's would support him in the battle. For all their friendly talk, Henry must have still harbored doubts about which way his supposed allies would go.

Records of deaths in the area on August 20 also indicate that there may have been some skirmishing between forces raised locally to fight for Richard and those allied to Henry. The records of the time make it hard to be sure, but with the armies increasingly close and Richard drawing support from all over the Midlands, such a clash seems likely.

Soldiers continued coming to Henry on August 21, including some recruited to fight for Richard. This at least gave the rebel leader some cause for good cheer, but that same day, Richard marched his army out of Leicester with banners waving and a coronet glinting on his head in a display of power and status. Knowing that Henry was at Atherstone, the King headed west along a route that would let him intercept the invaders if they were marching toward London and would lead the armies straight toward each other if Henry continued east.

When Richard's army made camp that night, his men and Henry's were within a few miles of each other. The time for battle had come.

Chapter 6: The Armies

The armies of the Wars of the Roses were not primarily made up of professional soldiers. The following century would see the emergence of professional standing armies as Europe began a military and political revolution, but in the 1480s, armies were still recruited as and when the need arose. The English government kept 1,000 troops garrisoning Calais and paid for a few hundred to be maintained in the northern border region, but most armies were led by noblemen and made up largely of tenants from their lands. These men were not keen to stay away from home for long, and even the richer nobles did not want to keep paying for their presence on an extended campaign. This was one of the reasons why the Wars of the Roses were marked by short campaigns in which the sides forced each other to pitch battle; no one could rely on the men and funds needed for a drawn out war.

In an era of amateur armies, the forces that met at Bosworth were relatively experienced. The core of Henry's army consisted of mercenaries, nearly half of them soldiers recently discharged from the French military base as Pont de l'Arche. These were men confident enough in their abilities or desperate enough for the money that they were willing to fight for a living. Richard, meanwhile, drew much of his support from northern England, a region where he had become popular while serving as governor during his brother's reign. The north was plagued by violence, due to both Scottish raiders and the feuding that had taken place between noble families in the region, and its soldiers had a reputation for looting and causing trouble. Richard himself had gained experience leading such men in an invasion of Scotland in 1482.

Richard was a more experienced soldier than Henry, and some of his men were battle hardened, but this experienced core were a minority among large levies of amateur troops from East Anglia, the southeast and London, as well as locally recruited forces. Thus, while Henry's army was primarily made up of men with some military experience, Richard's was not.

For over a hundred years, archers had made up the majority of England's fighting forces, and Bosworth Field was no exception. Their main job was to provide cover for the advancing men-at-arms and to break up enemy formations before an attack. Alongside them were infantrymen equipped with pole weapons and whatever pieces of armor they could afford. The armies were led, both strategically and in providing a well-equipped fighting elite, by the men-at-arms. These were the noblemen and wealth gentry, not all of them knighted but all equipped in the way we associate with medieval knights, being encased in plate armor. They often used horses to travel to battle but then fought on foot.

Cavalry played a part, including scouting ahead of the armies and giving them information about the surrounding terrain and movements of their opponents, and a cavalry charge could provide a decisive blow near the end of a battle when the infantry were already worn down. Richard held a group of armored cavalry in reserve, apparently for this purpose.

Though gunpowder weapons were not yet a decisive factor in battles, both sides had some with them. Richard's army, like many of the period, included a train of light artillery for battlefield use. This would be used to soften up the enemy before close quarters fighting began. He may also have had a few men carrying early handguns, and Henry certainly did.

Henry's force included something of an oddity: a group of Scottish soldiers led by Alexander

Bruce of Earlshall, John of Haddington and Henderson of Haddington. These soldiers had been serving in King Charles' army, and he now permitted them to return to Britain as part of Henry's invasion force. It was a gesture in keeping with Franco-Scottish relations during the period, which were defined by the auld alliance, a longstanding pact whereby the French and the Scots agreed to help each other in fighting the English.

The rebels may also have had one other thing that Richard's army didn't: pikes. These longer polearm weapons were increasingly popular on the continent but not used in the British Isles. Both the presence of French mercenaries and the tactics used indicate a strong continental influence on Henry's army, and it is possible that his troops had brought pikes with them, although no accounts from the period mention this.

It is impossible to be accurate about the number of men taking the field at Bosworth, but it is known that Henry was seriously outnumbered, and it is easier to make a better estimate of his force than Richard's. The details, as with all medieval battles, are hazy, but Henry seems to have had around 5,000 men, 4,000 of whom had come with him from France and a further 1,000 or so picked up along the way. The largest additions were those provided by Gilbert Talbot and Sir Richard Corbet, who each provided several hundred men. Around a tenth of this army was a core of exiles and rebel nobles, and the rest was primarily mercenaries together with some locally recruited troops.

If this had been a foreign war, there would have been better records for the royal army due to the documents used in recruitment, but as it is, historians can only estimate the size of Richard's force, which was arriving bit by bit from around the country. Given the proximity of the battle to the muster point at Leicester, some troops may even have joined the army during the battle, hurrying to arrive as they heard sounds of fighting. Such latecomers aside, it is likely that Richard had between 8,000-10,000 men, outnumbering his opponent nearly 2-1. Due to the speed with which they traveled, a large proportion of horsemen had probably reached the muster, and the army had a large vanguard of cavalry, infantry and archers.

Of course, there were not just two armies on the field at Bosworth but three. The Stanley's had still not committed to either side, and when Richard threatened to execute Lord Strange if Lord Stanley didn't support he King, Stanley replied that he had other sons. Still, they could not be absent from the field; at this point, joining the winning side would ensure them the favor of whoever became king, while siding with no one would ensure the animosity of the ruler they had failed to support. Thus, their army appeared on the field of battle.

Arriving as two separate forces, Lord Stanley brought around 5,000 men while Sir William's force was estimated at 3,000. Together, they outnumbered Henry and may have come close to matching Richard. The sight of this force, which as far as Richard or Henry knew might be on the other side, must have sent a chill through both of them.

While the armies were nominally led by Henry, Richard, or Stanley, they fought in locally recruited groups under the lords who had brought them to battle. Probably organized into groups of around 100 men, each soldier would have found himself fighting alongside many men he knew and had traveled to the muster with. Some groups wore similarly colored items or clothing to make them easily identifiable, whether the livery of their lord or matching hoods, but there was no standard uniform, so most would have looked like a motley, disheveled bunch. Heraldry was used to identify the knightly leaders and on banners, which identified individual units, provided rallying points, and served as a way for commanders to keep track of what was going on.

Those commanders would be crucial to the fight. King Richard had never led an army in a large battle, but he had led an invasion of Scotland and commanded troops under his brother earlier in the Wars of the Roses. He was a smart and experienced commander. Henry, on the other hand, had no military experience, so he relied on the veteran John de Vere, Earl of Oxford, who commanded his vanguard and seems to have defined the rebel tactics. Oxford was a veteran of earlier battles in the Wars of the Roses, had continued to fight as a privateer while living in exile, and had even escaped from captivity at Hammes Castle near Calais. Like Richard, he brought years of experience to the field of battle.

Chapter 7: Initial Maneuvers

To the medieval mind, a battle was more than just a clash between mortal men. The idea of trial by battle, and the deep connection between religion and politics, meant that the outcomes of such fights were often seen as granted by God. To soldiers on both sides, the case between Richard III and Henry Tudor would be tried not in court but on a muddy field, with the Almighty as judge and jury, but as it turned out, the critical intercession would come not from the Lord on High but from the Lord Stanley.

A deeply pious man, Richard was awake by dawn on August 22, 1485, and he ordered that his army be provided with both breakfast and a holy service. This religious element was normal for armies going into battle at the time, both because of the perceived divine element in war's outcome and because of the need to care for the souls of men who might be about to die.

Henry's army also rose with the dawn and prepared for battle, and the two armies marched toward each other across the land around Fenn Lane, which would provide Henry's route east toward Leicester. The exact site of the battle was long uncertain to historians, but recent archaeological evidence indicates its location near what was then a small marsh called Fenn Hole, just to the south of Fenn Lane. Fenn Hole provided one end of the battle lines, and Richard anchored his army's left flank against the marsh to the south, making it difficult for his enemies to outflank him from that direction. His troops blocked the road, and thus Henry's route east, with the bulk of the royal army north of Fenn Lane and the armored cavalry reserve to the rear.

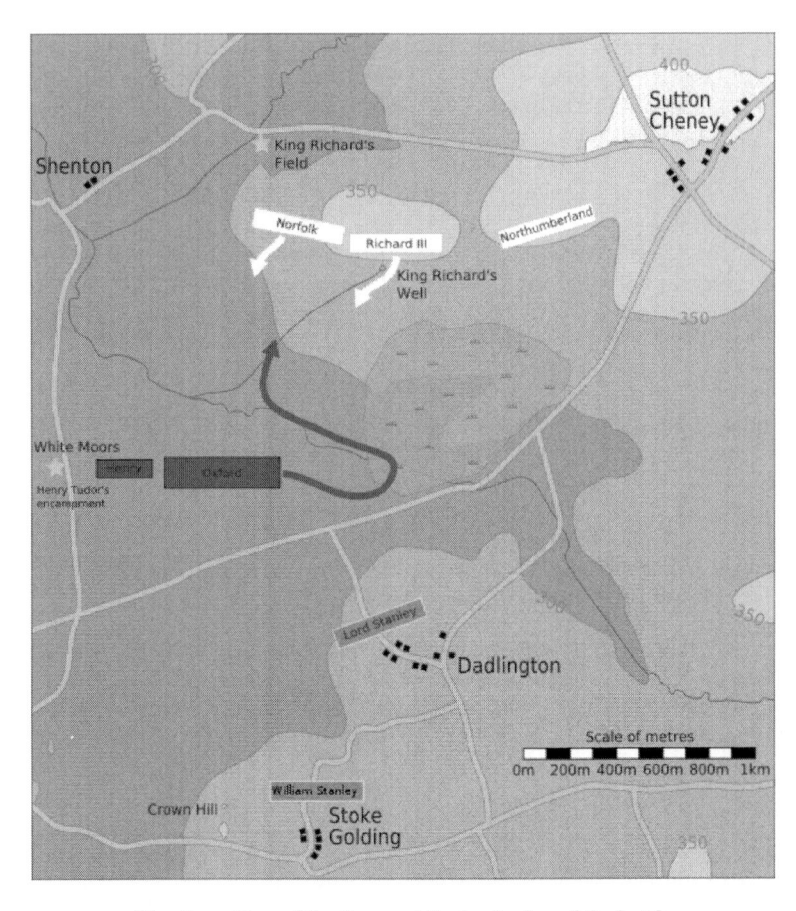

The disposition of the forces at the beginning of the battle

Rodney Burton's picture of Richard's Well

Richard spread his vanguard out to create a long line, giving him two advantages. First, it would be difficult for the rebels to outflank him at either end. Second, he might hope to wrap the ends of his line around the enemy, enveloping them and bringing his superior numbers to bear. With Richard thus arrayed, Henry had no choice but to face him; he could not travel east without a fight, and if he carried on southeast towards London, then Richard's larger force could pursue him and attack him in the rear. He therefore sent a message to his supposed ally, Lord Stanley, asking him to join forces. Stanley, sticking with the strategy that had seen him through the campaign so far, found excuses not to commit in this way, thus keeping his troops separate. He may have sent a few knights and their followers to bolster Henry's force, but if he did so, it was a purely token gesture.

Henry's plan had relied on having the Stanley's on his side. Without them he needed to think again, and he needed to do it fast. Starting three miles from Richard's position, Henry marched his men across the ground around Fenn Lane, stopping about 800 yards from the King's army (and thus out of range of bowshot). There, he formed up his army with its right flank protected by Fenn Hole and with Fenn Lane running through their center. His line was inevitably thinner than Richard's, so rather than forming up in the traditional medieval way in three formations (known as battles), the army was instead organized as a single formation. This was almost certainly done at the instigation of the Earl of Oxford, who in turn was influenced by the military writer Christine of Pizan. Christine of Pizan recommended such a formation for smaller armies and had cited examples of its past success.

Now close enough to see the gleam of their enemies' weapons, the soldiers donned their helmets and prepared to fight. Archery and gunfire announced the start of the battle, with each side bombarding the opposing formation to weaken them before the real fighting began.

The battle for England's crown was underway, and to the southeast, beyond Fenn Hole, the Stanley armies watched and waited.

Chapter 8: The Climax

Following the initial exchange of missiles, the two armies finally clashed up close. Richard's vanguard attacked but was held in place by Henry's smaller vanguard, commanded by the Earl of Oxford. Shortly after the fighting had begun, Oxford put his plan for the battle into action; on his order, the rebels moved into tight formation, the men of each unit gathering together within 10 feet of their standard. In doing so, many of them pulled back from the press of the melee, and the royalists, fearing some kind of trap, did not press forward.

There was a lull in the fighting, during which Oxford formed his men up into wedge formations. Fighting in wedges, like the use of pikes, was a relatively new approach to warfare that was becoming popular in continental Europe. Usually supported by pikes on the flanks, wedge formations hit hard and tried to punch a hole through the enemy line.

Advancing from the rebel left flank, these formations came as a surprise to the Yorkists. Between their military experience and their novel tactics, the rebels had gained a crucial edge, balancing out the superior numbers of the enemy, preventing them from bringing those numbers to bear, and creating a brutal, protracted melee in which the mercenaries' superior experience would act in their favor. When they broke through the Yorkist formation, they were now able to attack them not just from the front but from the right and the rear.

The royal vanguard, now heavily engaged with Oxford's forces, was led by John Howard, Duke of Norfolk. Like Oxford, Norfolk was a veteran of the Wars of the Roses, and the two men were old rivals who had fought on opposite sides in battle and competed for control of the same lands. In fact, following Oxford's exile, Norfolk held much property that had once been Oxford's. Norfolk had risen through the ranks in service to the House of York; after serving King Richard's brother, Edward IV, Norfolk was given his dukedom by Richard, to whom he was a friend and loyal adherent.

Howard

Norfolk's experience had stood him in good stead in the past, but at Bosworth Field it was not enough. The faceguard on his helmet had been torn off in the melee, and an arrow subsequently came crashing through his face, killing him in the midst of the battle and leaving the royal vanguard without their commander.

The death of Norfolk created a dangerous moment for Richard. Losing the commander of the vanguard could damage the army's morale, as well as their tactical coherence, so something was needed to swing the battle back Richard's way. As a result, the King found himself looking for an opportunity as the battle reached its climax.

At the height of the battle, Henry found himself isolated from the main body of his army. He and his bodyguards may have been heading toward the Stanley forces in the hope of bringing them in on his side, or they may simply have been separated from the main bulk of the army as it advanced. Whatever, the case, they were certainly not committed to the main fighting, the inexperienced Henry having left this in the hands of his commanders.

Through a gap in the battle lines, Richard spotted the usurper flying his royal banners, and indignation at the sight may have further riled the King, who was already looking for an opportunity to deliver a counter-punch to end the rebel advance. The sight of Henry separated from his army seemed to offer the chance to deliver a decisive blow.

Charging at the head of his reserve of heavy cavalry, Richard galloped toward the nemesis looking to replace him as king. This reserve was a force of a few hundred men made up of bodyguards and members of the royal household, and had been held back for just such an opportunity. In the warfare of the period, a bold strike by a small group of heavy cavalry could sometimes swing the tide of battle or be used to chase down important enemies as they attempted to escape. If Richard could reach the Tudor pretender, then he could remove the head from the enemy army, destroying their morale, ensuring his victory, and permanently ending Henry's threat to the crown. This was a courageous move by the Yorkist King. His whole army was not yet committed to the fight, but the tide of battle was going against them, and he was thus risking himself and those close to him in a gamble that he could decapitate the opposition.

It was a moment of high drama, and the stuff that chivalric legends were made of. The Yorkist king galloped out of the side of his own lines followed by a formation of knights in full plate armor, their heraldic colors flapping in the wind. Henry, defended by his own mounted guards and some of the French infantry, was unable to retreat and stood resolute, ready to face his opponent. As Richard ploughed into the rebel force, he cut down Sir William Brandon, Henry's standard bearer, casting aside the Lancastrian colors. Faced with the towering figure of Sir John Cheyne, he also beat this knight, knocking him to the ground. As Henry stood in the center of a knot of soldiers, Richard and his men pressed ever forward, cutting a bloody swathe through the rebel leader's defenders.

Facing each other with their small bands of armed men, both claimants to the throne showed courage and decisiveness, but it was at this moment that Sir William Stanley also acted boldly (at least by the standards of his family): he chose a side. Seeing Richard and Henry locked in battle just downhill from him, Sir William took his men to support Henry.

It is interesting to note that it was Sir William and not Lord Stanley who now led his men into battle, though William certainly already had the least to lose. Declared a traitor by Richard, his future was far from secure if the House of York won. Was he simply the most eager to take part, or was there more to it than this? Were the Stanley's once again hedging their bets? Did Lord Stanley, who according to one chronicler ordered Sir William's charge, hold himself back so that, if Richard somehow made a comeback, he could join the King's side with his larger force? Was he still trying to bet both ways on a two horse race? Or did he simply not want to commit his troops too early, instead letting others do the bulk of the fighting for him?

The answer will never be clear, but Sir William Stanley's intervention proved to be the decisive moment. Upon their arrival, Richard was outnumbered and quickly surrounded. He had the opportunity to flee, and those close by urged him to, but he was determined to win or die trying. Perhaps he believed that to lose would be to die anyway; if he ran, his army was likely to collapse, and once he had lost the initiative, Henry Tudor would become King, with access to England's military and legal resources. How long then before Richard was hunted down and killed?

Whatever drove him on, Richard fought to the end, and was killed in the thick of the fighting. Eventually unhorsed, his helmet was removed by his opponents and he was killed by one of two heavy blows to the back of the head - one probably delivered by a sword, the other by a halberd. Several men later claimed to have struck the fatal blow - Rhys ap Thomas, Ralph Rudyard of Staffordshire and an anonymous Welsh halberdier among them. Whoever did the deed, the King was dead.

Even those who sided with Henry recognized the courage and vigor with which Richard fought. Polydore Vergil, Henry's court historian, described how "king Richard alone was killed fighting manfully in the thickest press of his enemies... his courage was high and fierce and failed him not even at the death which, when his men forsook him, he preferred to take by the sword rather than, by foul flight, to prolong his life."

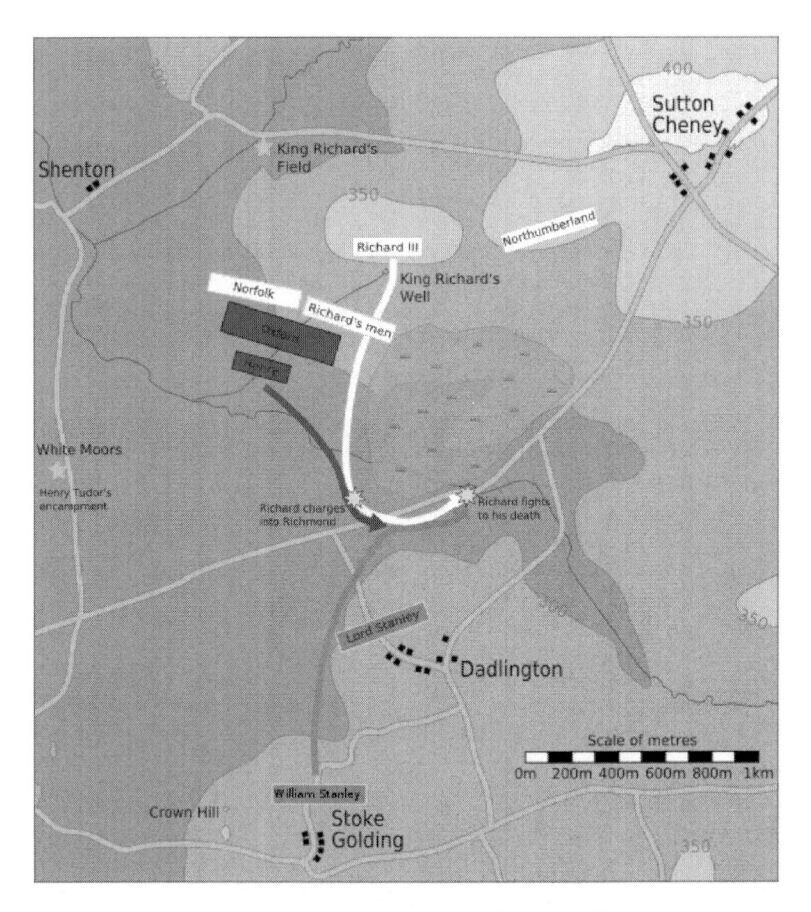

A map showing the spot where Richard fell

As news of the King's death spread, his army, already faring badly against Oxford, finally broke. Some turned and ran, while others threw down their arms and surrendered. As was the way in medieval battle, many were probably killed as they tried to run, the victors not wanting to give them a chance to regroup and fight again.

Henry, doubtless relieved to have been saved from Richard's attack, gave thanks to God for his triumph. He then ascended the nearest hill and addressed his troops, commending them for their victory and ordering that the wounded be tended and the dead buried. He thanked his commanders and knighted several men who had brought troops to the battle, including Rhys ap Thomas and Gilbert Talbot. Amid jubilant cries of "God save the King!," Lord Stanley took the coronet that Richard had worn into battle and placed it on Henry's head. The Stanley's were, in every sense of the phrase, the kingmakers of Bosworth Field.

A depiction of Lord Stanley presenting Richard III's crown to Henry

As for Richard of York, his body was carried away naked on the back of a horse and then left on public display for two days to prove that he was dead. He was then buried with relatively little ceremony in a place of honor at Grey Friars church in Leicester. The church was later destroyed during the Reformation, and with the Tudors still in power, no one took care to find a new home for Richard's remains. They remained hidden until discovered by archaeologists in 2012 and reburied with great ceremony in 2015. Richard III finally received a funeral fit for a king.

Chapter 9: The Aftermath of the Battle

By fulfilling his promise to marry Elizabeth of York, Henry ensured the security of his regime, as their marriage on January 18, 1486 unified the Houses of Lancaster and York. Instead of either of these families' titles, the newly installed line would be known as the Tudors, and they took as their emblem a rose that included both the red of Lancaster and the white of York, symbolically combining the heraldry of the two houses.

Henry also took steps to bring Richard's supporters into line behind him. By backdating his reign to the day before Bosworth Field, he threatened them with potential trial for treason, but he also held out an olive branch, saying that anyone who swore loyalty to him would be safe no matter what side they had taken.

Learning from the experience of the Wars of the Roses, he increased royal power while reducing that of the nobility, with the aim of preventing future revolts and civil wars. It was a shift in power that would contribute to the strong central rule for which the Tudors were known, and which became important across Europe in the following centuries.

Still, the fighting was not quite over. Henry had imprisoned the other remaining claimant to the throne: the young Earl of Warwick, son of George, Duke of Clarence. In 1487, a group of Yorkist rebels convinced a commoner named Lambert Simnel to impersonate Warwick and claim to have escaped from the Tower. With an army of English rebels and Irish and German mercenaries, this group tried to seize the throne, but Henry VII crushed their army at the Battle of Stoke on June 16, regarded by many as the last battle of the Wars of the Roses. The Earl of Lincoln, who led the plot, died in battle, while Simnel was pardoned and given a job in the royal kitchens.

Henry would face other pretenders and attempted uprisings, but none of them were even as effective as the Simnel plot. While their consequences would echo down through history, the Wars of the Roses were effectively over.

The Wars of the Roses were a period of huge upheaval among England's ruling class, and the impact they had on the country was nearly unprecedented. The nearest comparable periods of civil war were the Anarchy of 1135-1154, in which King Stephen and the Empress Matilda grappled for control of England, and the English Civil Wars of 1642-1651, in which Parliament battled with Charles I and his successor Charles II.

Next to those two, the Wars of the Roses were by far the lesser evil; both the Anarchy and the Civil Wars have gone down in history as periods of huge and bloody turmoil, with social and political instability, a damaged economy, and death and disorder affecting everyone from the top to the bottom of society across large swathes of England and the territories it controlled. The Wars of the Roses, on the other hand, kept the violence self-contained. Few towns or castles were besieged, and this is reflected in the fact that defenses were not rebuilt specially for the wars. Without sieges, the populations of these towns suffered neither the hardships of starvation nor the chaos of a sacking that often followed. Similarly, land was not pillaged by the armies. Both sides were aiming to be seen as fair and rightful rulers, so did not want to harm their subjects. For the most part, regions did not commit to one side or the other, so they avoided bringing punishment down on their heads.

Swift, decisive military campaigns followed by political resolution meant that there were not the drawn out effects of other wars, such as a drain on the national economy or the impact of raiding and counter-raiding. The Wars of the Roses never directly touched areas such as East Anglia or the Cornish Peninsula, and they did not involve or affect most of the lower and middle classes. Work, trade, and farming all continued, and if anything, the rule of Henry VI proved so weak that the reigns of Edward IV and Richard III brought greater peace and prosperity for many. In short, except for those fighting the war, there was little disruption.

Among the upper classes, it was a different story, with bloody instability taking many lives but ultimately leading to little long term change. Many noblemen died in the fighting, and while most fell on the battlefield, plenty were executed or murdered while in captivity. The conflict was one between noble factions vying for supremacy, and it was in their interests to see each other permanently and violently removed. The disappearance of the Princes in the Tower, though particularly poignant, must have come as less of a shock to people who had seen their family, friends and acquaintances die. Both sides were made up of the same social, political and economic elite, and even the people they killed were often people they knew in person.

Despite the weight of personal loss, there were few losses to the political system. Noble houses died out, particularly those at the center of the conflict, but accidents, disease, military careers and lack of heirs meant that as many noble houses disappeared during the preceding period as during the war itself. If the lines of Lancaster and York could keep finding heirs to throw into the political grinder, then so could the families following them. The names might have changed, but the aristocracy that emerged from the Wars of the Roses looked almost identical to the one at the beginning.

For the monarchy, this was a period of upheaval, but the ultimate result was renewed stability. The upheaval began not with the outbreak of war but with the overthrow of Richard II, which created competing claims to the throne. Without a strong ruler, there was nothing to hold back the ambitions of competing nobles, ambitions they legitimized by backing a competing claim to the throne. By taking firm control and marrying Elizabeth of York, Henry Tudor ended both sources of the disturbance. The competing claims had been brought back together, and an effective ruler sat on the throne.

It was this effective ruler who oversaw the biggest long term effect of the war: a reduction in the military and political power of the nobility. Noble power had fueled the war, and Henry understandably sought to take it away. He brought in laws against livery and maintenance, the system by which nobles had assembled their armies, and military power was increasingly the king's to wield directly.

The changes brought by the Wars of the Roses were the English embodiment of wider changes in Western Europe in the late 15th and 16th centuries. Political and military power was increasingly centralized in the hands of monarchs at the expense of the nobility, and to prevent conflict between those nobles. This led to stronger national armies. At the same time, the merchant classes were very slowly becoming more powerful at the expense of the aristocracy. The fact that the Wars of the Roses disrupted the nobility but not the merchants perhaps assisted in their ascent, but if it did then it was just a small part of a wider trend.

For all their blood and infamy, the Wars of the Roses simply brought England back onto the course it was already taking.

Online Resources

The Wars of the Roses: The History of the Conflicts that Brought the Tudors to Power in England by Charles River Editors

History of the Life and Reign of Richard the Third by James Gairdner

The Houses of Lancaster and York by James Gairdner

The War of the Roses by J.G. Edgar

The War of the Roses by R.B. Mowat

Bibliography

Baldwin, David (2002). Elizabeth Woodville. Stroud, Gloucestershire: Sutton Publishing. ISBN 0-7509-2774-7.

Goodwin, George (2012). Fatal Colours. Phoenix. ISBN 978-0-7538-2817-5.

Haigh, Philip A. (1995). The Military Campaigns of the Wars of the Roses. ISBN 0-7509-0904-8.

Lander, J.R. (1980). Government and Community: England, 1450–1509. Cambridge: Harvard University Press. ISBN 0-674-35794-9.

Peverley, Sarah L. (2004). "66:1". Adapting to Readeption in 1470–1471: The Scribe as Editor in a Unique Copy of John Hardyng's Chronicle of England (Garrett MS. 142). The Princeton University Library Chronicle. pp. 140–72.

Goodwin, George (2012). Fatal Colours. London: Phoenix. ISBN 978-0-7538-2817-5.

Pollard, A.J. (1988). The Wars of the Roses. Basingstoke: Macmillan Education. ISBN 0-333-40603-6.

Redstone, Vincent B. (1902). "Social Conditions of England during the Wars of the Roses". Royal Historical Society 16 (1).

Rowse, A.L. (1966). Bosworth Field & the Wars of the Roses. Wordsworth Military Library.

ISBN 1-85326-691-4.

Royle, Trevor (2009). The Road to Bosworth Field. London: Little, Brown. ISBN 978-0-316-72767-9.

Sadler, John (2011). Towton: The Battle of Palm Sunday Field 1461. Barnsley: Pen and Sword Military. ISBN 978-1-84415-965-9.

Seward, Desmond (1995). A Brief History of the Wars of the Roses. London: Constable & Co. ISBN 978-1-84529-006-1.

Wagner, John A. (2001). Encyclopedia of the Wars of the Roses. ABC-Clio. ISBN 1-85109-358-3.

Wise, Terence; Embleton, G.A. (1983). The Wars of the Roses. London: Osprey Military. ISBN 0-85045-520-0.

Printed in Great Britain
by Amazon.co.uk, Ltd.,
Marston Gate.